I Know That!

Farm Animals

Claire Llewellyn

SEA-TO-SEA
Mankato Collingwood London

This edition first published in 2005 by
Sea-to-Sea Publications
1980 Lookout Drive
North Mankato
Minnesota 56003

Copyright © Sea-to-Sea Publications 2005
Text copyright © Claire Llewellyn 2005

ISBN 1-932889-33-7

Printed in China

Library of Congress Control Number: 2004103733

2 4 6 8 9 7 5 3

Published by arrangement with the Watts Publishing Group Ltd, London

Educational advisor: Gill Matthews, nonfiction literacy consultant and Inset trainer
Editor: Rachel Cooke
Series design: Peter Scoulding
Designer: James Marks
Acknowledgements: J C Allen/FLPA: 19. Ian Beames/Ecoscene: 21. Frank Blackburn/Ecoscene: 20. Andrew Brown/
Ecoscene: 8. Mark Edwards/Still Pictures: 4, 22c. Eye Ubiquitous: 11. Pierre Gleizes/Still Pictures: 9. Paul Glendell/
Still Pictures: 13b. Chinch Gryniewicz/Ecoscene: 12, 22b. Angela Hampton/Ecoscene: 1, 2, 5, 14b, 16. Anthony
Harrison/Ecoscene: 10. Hubert Klein/Still Pictures: 15. Joy Michaud/Ecoscene: front cover, 6. Thomas Raupach/Still
Pictures: 7b. Roland Seitre/Still Pictures: 18, 23cr. David Wootton/Ecoscene: 17, 23bl. Harry Cory-Wright: 14c, 23tl.

Contents

Living on a farm

Many animals live on farms.
Farmers give animals food and shelter.

Farmers help animals care for their babies.

There are farms all over the country. Some of them are even in towns. Where is your nearest farm?

A herd of cows

Many farmers keep cows.
Cows give us milk and meat.

A calf drinks milk from its mother.

Farmers milk cows twice a day.

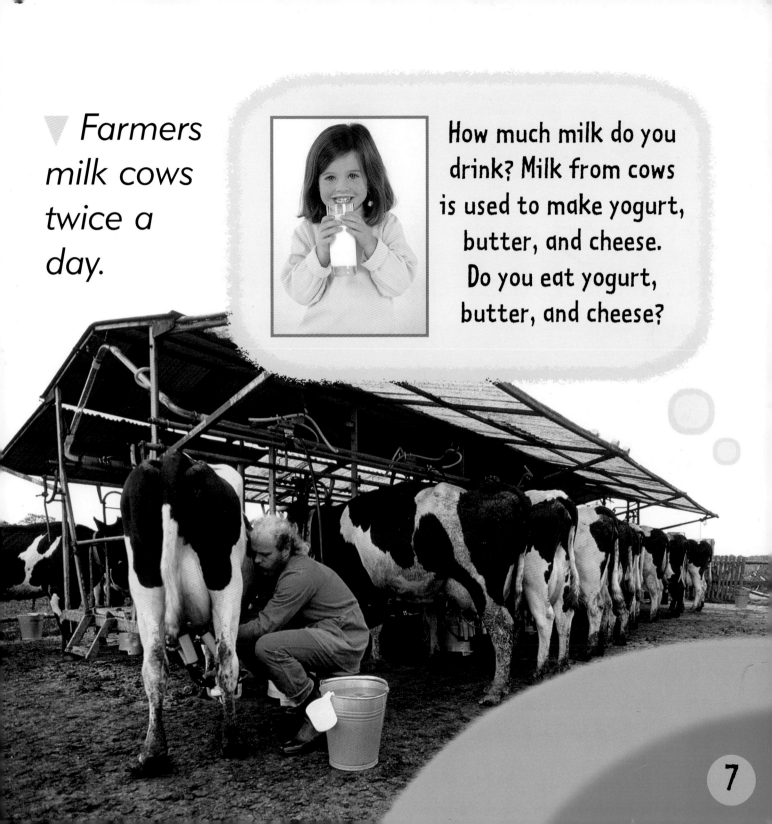

How much milk do you drink? Milk from cows is used to make yogurt, butter, and cheese. Do you eat yogurt, butter, and cheese?

Field or barn?

For most of the year, cows live in fields. In winter, they are kept in barns.

▲ *In the field, cows graze on grass.*

In the barn, the farmer gives the cows their food.

A cow is a female animal. The male is called a bull. A cow's baby is called a calf. We call all these animals "cattle."

A flock of sheep

Many farmers keep sheep. Sheep give us wool, meat, and milk.

▶ *Sheep have one or two lambs in the spring.*

A sheepdog helps to move sheep around the farm.

A female sheep is called a ewe. A male sheep is called a ram. A baby sheep is called a lamb.

A warm coat

Sheep have a wooly coat that keeps them warm.

▼ *Sheep can live outside all year round.*

▼ *A sheep's coat is cut every year.*

We use sheep's wool to make clothes like sweaters, hats, scarves, and gloves. What do woolen things feel like?

Keeping chickens

Some farmers keep chickens. They give us eggs and meat.

▼ Some chickens are kept outside.

▼ Chickens' eggs are good to eat.

A female chicken is called a hen. The male is called a rooster. A baby is called a chick.

◀ *Some chickens are kept in cages.*

15

Keeping pigs

Some farmers keep pigs. They give us meat such as bacon and ham.

A female pig is called a sow. The male is called a boar. A baby pig is called a piglet.

▼ Most pigs are kept inside.

◄ Some pigs live outside. They shelter in pigsties.

Other farm animals

Other animals live on farms. They help the farmer in different ways.

Cats catch mice and rats.

Some farmers keep horses to ride.

There are many farm animals in this book. Can you think of any others?

Wild animals

Many wild animals live on farms. Farms give them food and shelter.

▶ *Birds nest in the barns.*

Farmers shut chickens up at night to try to keep them safe from foxes.

◀Foxes take a chicken if they can.

I know that...

1 Many animals live on farms.

2 Farmers give animals food and shelter.

3 Cows give us milk and meat.

4 Sheep give us wool, milk, and meat.

5 Chickens give us meat and eggs.

6 Pigs give us meat.

7 Cats, dogs, and horses also live on farms.

8 Some wild animals make their homes on farms.

Index

About this book

I Know That! is designed to introduce children to the process of gathering information and using reference books, one of the key skills needed to begin more formal learning at school. For this reason, each book's structure reflects the information books children will use later in their learning career—with key information in the main text and additional facts and ideas in the captions. The panels give an opportunity for further activities, ideas, or discussions. The contents page and index are helpful reference guides.

The language is carefully chosen to be accessible to children just beginning to read. Illustrations support the text but also give information in their own right; active consideration and discussion of images is another key referencing skill. The main aim of the series is to build confidence—showing children how much they already know and giving them the ability to gather new information for themselves. With this in mind, the *I know that...* section at the end of the book is a simple way for children to revisit what they already know as well as what they have learned from reading the book.